Flood Tide

Flood Tide
Opening the Windows Of Heaven

by
Oral Roberts

HARRISON HOUSE
Tulsa, Oklahoma

Unless otherwise indicated,
all Scripture quotations are from
the *King James Version* of the Bible.

Copyright © 1981
by
Oral Roberts
Tulsa, Oklahoma
74171

Published by
Harrison House, Inc.
P.O. Box 35035
Tulsa, Oklahoma 74135
ISBN 0-89274-191-0
Printed in the United States
All Rights Reserved

Foreword

For many, many years my life and ministry have been blessed by the deep spiritual teachings of Oral Roberts. Decades before it became a popular teaching, this great man of God began telling the masses that God wants them well and healthy, and that He wants them to prosper.

I believe God has used him more than any other man of our day to awaken the Church to these truths. Through Oral's unique ministry, countless souls have been saved, thousands have been healed through the power of God, and many more have learned from him biblical truths they never knew existed.

Today, Oral Roberts is a living legend. He has dared to follow a vision of God, in spite of the countless attacks of Satan that have been leveled against him and the City of Faith. But he has stood firm; and today the City of Faith is becoming reality, offering the best hope of "whole person healing" to millions!

Yet for all his fame, Oral has remained a compassionate, sensitive, caring man. In these last few years, Tammy and I have had the honor of becoming close friends with Oral and Evelyn. Their kindness to us has meant so much.

Just as an example of the kind of man he is, several months ago Oral flew to Charlotte, North Carolina, to help us when PTL had a need... in spite of the fact that the City of Faith was desperately needing money. But he was practicing what he preaches — he preferred his brother over himself, in spite of his own need, by giving out of his need. I can't express how much that meant to us.

Oral has given us advice, a shoulder to cry on, a sympathetic ear, and encouraging words from the Lord. On numerous occasions, he has ministered to us unselfishly with his time.

And every time I am with him, I am even more awed by his knowledge and his depth in the Word. He is indeed an anointed man of God.

This new book, *Flood Tide*, is another sample of his powerful teachings. In his clear and simple style,

Oral details how to open the "flood tides" of blessings in your life.

Each step is backed up with direct quotes from the Bible, and every thought is clearly defined. Whether you are a newborn Christian, or one who has walked with God all your life, you will find this exciting book rich in understanding of God's principles.

I pray that you will not only read this book, but that you will put it to the test. It can literally change your life!

Oral Roberts has done it again with this great book... and I know God will continue to bless him for his obedience!

                        Love,
                        Jim Bakker
President, PTL Television Network
Charlotte, North Carolina

Contents

Introduction

1	Back To Beginnings	19
2	The Blessing	29
3	God's Chosen People	39
4	"Return Unto Me"	51
5	God Is Our Deliverer	67
6	Tithing In The Seed-Faith Way	81
7	Flood Tide	103
8	The Devourer Rebuked In Your Life	125
9	Christianity — The Great Confession	135

The Ministry Of Oral Roberts   141

God Anointed Me To Write Flood Tide For You

I am writing *Flood Tide* under a powerful anointing of the Lord, a strong leading to minister more of the faith of God to the faith you already have. To get you into faith so God will open the windows of heaven until you are in the *Flood Tide* of His blessings — spiritually, physically, financially — is why this book was born.

I know God hurts with you when you are not acting in faith and you suffer lack of the very blessing He has prepared for you. I know, because He has put that hurt in me for you.

It's amazing how when I feel what God feels concerning you, He begins to flood my mind with a deeper understanding of the Word of God to share with you. I am absolutely convinced the answer to all your problems is in His Word as men like myself

Flood Tide

minister it to you, and as you read and study and apply it to the everyday things of your life.

It has been a joy to write this book because I had spent months and months preaching the concepts and principles of it to people by the tens of thousands, as well as to small groups and individuals. Also, I had applied every part of it to my life and discovered it causes the wonders of God to happen today just as in Bible times.

I am very concerned for you, especially that you will go to heaven when you leave this world. And I'm very concerned that between now and that moment, you will learn what God tells you to do — then do it — for Him to open the windows and actually **pour** you out **blessings** that will truly **overflow** your life.

Then you will know God with the same faith of Abraham, who was **blessed** and **made a blessing.**

You will receive the spiritual union with God you have dreamed of. You will experience the exhilarating power of God — supernaturally and naturally — for your *health*. And you will begin to have a completely new understanding of how to prosper in your *finances* from all the gold and silver God originally placed on this earth for the people who believe and obey Him — and who give their best in their labor.

Flood Tide

As you read this book, chapter by chapter, word for word, and feel yourself building to a climax of personally reaching *Flood Tide*, I am expecting you to trust God for things you never even knew He had. I am expecting you to experience just what it means to know God is opening the windows of heaven to **you**, while you are still on this earth. It's going to be a great experience for you, just as it is for me already.

— Oral Roberts

Bring ye all the tithes into the storehouse, that there may be meat in mine house, and prove me now herewith, saith the Lord of hosts, if I will not open you the windows of heaven, and pour you out a blessing, that there shall not be room enough to receive it.

And I will rebuke the devourer for your sakes, and he shall not destroy the fruits of your ground; neither shall your vine cast her fruit before the time in the field, saith the Lord of hosts.

Malachi 3:10,11

Flood Tide
Opening the Windows Of Heaven

1
Back To Beginnings

"He (Abraham) believed in the Lord; and he counted it to him for righteousness."
                                              Genesis 15:6

1
Back To Beginnings

"...the blockers, beloved in the truth,
and he counted it to him for righteousness."
Genesis 15:6

...

...the kingdom of the heavens...
...by the blood of the...
...the inmost working tower today.

Chapter 1
Back To Beginnings

If you want to know where you are and where you are going, you have to go back to your beginnings.

Where did we come from?
Who started it all?

Consider Abraham, the father of all who are of faith. We can search our beginnings and trace our lives from Abraham to this very moment.

Most people don't know Abraham at all — the kind of life he lived before God or the kind of God he knew.

Because they do not know the God that Abraham served, they have no way of bringing themselves into harmony with the Lord and with His miracle-working power today.

Flood Tide

As long as they are without a relationship with God today, tomorrow will have no meaning for them. They will not know they are blessed rather than cursed, delivered rather than bound in captivity.

Every day millions of people get up in the morning with no purpose for the day. They understand nothing about today and have no vision of tomorrow or of the world to come.

Their present is without meaning.

Their past is as though it never happened.

"God" is just a curse word or a byword — *something* or *someone* that has no reality to their existence.

They see themselves as being left on their own — not knowing who they are, where they came from, or where they are going.

This is the condition of the human race at this moment.

Well, friend, the Bible is the Word of God. It holds the answer to all our questions. It tells us who we are, where we came from, and where we are headed.

OUR FAITH BEGINNINGS

In the New Testament, Galatians chapter 3, St. Paul takes us back to our faith beginnings.

In verses 6 and 7, he writes:

Even as Abraham believed God, and it was accounted to him for righteousness.

Know ye therefore that they which are of faith, the same are the children of Abraham.

This is an exciting statement: Abraham believed God and, because of his believing, was seen by God as righteous. Therefore, they which are of faith (that's you and me!) are the children of Abraham.

We who have faith in God — a faith that is alive and vital — are *covered* by the righteousness of God. When God looks at us, He does not see the things we have done wrong in the past. All those things have been repented of and washed away by the blood of Jesus. We stand righteous in the sight of God. Something good has happened to us . . . and continues to happen.

Galatians 3:29 says, *And if ye be Christ's, then are ye Abraham's seed, and heirs according to the promise.* If we belong to Christ, we are of the *seed* of Abraham — and that makes us heirs to the promise God gave to Abraham *and to his seed.*

Our Jewish friends claim to be heirs of Abraham, and they have a great right to claim it because of their heritage going back to their father, Abraham. But most of them have missed Christ. At least, they have missed Him so far.

We are the descendants of Abraham — not by birth as the Jews are, but by an act of faith in God. We have been grafted in. By our faith in Jesus Christ, we have been made "reborn" sons and daughters of Abraham.

Abraham is so valuable to us today. Our faith as Christians began with him.

Abraham was the first man to have faith that went beyond himself. When Abraham heard the voice of God, he obeyed what God told him to do. He recognized who God really was. He gave tithes of everything to the Lord.

Abraham was the first man to totally believe the Lord; and because of his faith, the Lord covered Abraham with His own righteousness.

ADAM TO NOAH

In the beginning when God created the world, He created the first man, Adam, and spoke to him. But Adam did not really hear what God was saying. He turned his back on God.

Adam's "sin," or disobedience, caused Abraham and his descendants (all of mankind) to lose paradise — which represented the goodness of God. As a result of Adam's disobedience, a curse came upon the earth.

In the ten generations from Adam to Noah, there was so much sin in the world; but the glory of God given to Adam still had its power over the earth.

The glory of the Creator had not been completely erased, even though it had been refused and cast aside. Consequently, sickness had not yet taken free root upon the earth, and Adam's body — so wondrously made by God — remained well throughout his lifetime, which spanned a period of 900 years.

Then when Noah was born into the earth, he like Abraham was a man who believed God's Word. On the authority of God's Word alone, he moved by faith and built an ark to save the human race from a flood that covered the whole earth.

Flood Tide

Still, we can find no evidence of sickness in Noah's family or in the various types of animals that were taken aboard the ark. Even with an abundance of sin in the world, sickness had not as yet taken dominance.

MAN-MADE GODS

By the time of Abraham, the world had put down the one true God and had created other gods in His place.

Why did the people create these other gods?

To satisfy their spiritual hunger.

God built something of Himself within all of mankind: We are incurably religious and spiritual. We have an insatiable desire to seek after something greater than ourselves.

When mankind turned from the one true God, they still had to satisfy their spiritual hunger. So they made other gods.

Because of their built-in desire to look up to God, they placed these man-made idols on the highest hills and mountains.

They did everything possible to make these gods real, but their efforts were futile. Any gods made by human hands will have no life.

> Surely he cuts cedars for himself, and takes a cypress or an oak, and raises it for himself among the trees of the forest. He plants a fir, and the rain makes it grow.
>
> Then it becomes something for a man to burn, so he takes one of them and warms himself; he also makes a fire to bake bread. He also makes a god and worships it; he makes it a graven image, and falls down before it.
>
> Half of it he burns in the fire; over this half he eats meat as he roasts a roast, and is satisfied. He also warms himself and says, "Aha! I am warm, I have seen the fire."
>
> But the rest of it he makes into a god, his graven image. He falls down before it and worships; he also prays to it and says, "Deliver me, for thou are my god."
>
> Isaiah 44:14-17 N.A.S.

THEN CAME ABRAHAM

Then there came one man who turned away from worshipping these graven images.

Flood Tide

That man was Abraham.

He refused to bow before these man-made images and worship them as "God."

Of all the thousands of gods made by man and placed on the high hills of the earth, there was one God above them all. The most high God. Possessor of heaven and earth. Deliverer from all our enemies. The one true God. The living God.

Abraham believed in this God!

This is where it all began.

2
The Blessing

"In thee shall all families
of the earth be blessed."
Genesis 12:3

Chapter 2
The Blessing

Abraham believed in the one true God.

He believed that his God would deliver him from the hands of his enemies — and he proved it!

In the 14th chapter of Genesis, we read how Abraham's nephew Lot and his family, who lived in the wicked city of Sodom, were captured and carried off by an enemy army.

Abraham did not agree with Lot's life style in Sodom. But because he was a righteous man, Abraham wanted to rescue his kinsman. He gathered his 318 men and pursued this enemy army all the way to Damascus. He whipped that army, though it was much larger in number, and brought back his loved ones, plus all the loot that had been taken.

Flood Tide

When Abraham returned in victory, he was met by the high priest, Melchizedek. We read from the 14th chapter of Genesis, verses 18-20:

> *And Melchizedek king of Salem brought forth bread and wine: and he was the priest of the most high God.*
>
> *And he blessed him, and said, Blessed be Abraham of the most high God, possessor of heaven and earth:*
>
> *And blessed be the most high God, which hath delivered thine enemies into thy hand. And he gave him tithes of all.*

When Abraham returned from his victory, two very important things happened:
Melchizedek, king of Salem and priest of God, pronounced a blessing on Abraham's life.
Abraham gave tithes of all to the priest of God.

THE BLESSING WITH PROMISE

Melchizedek, the priest of God, came out to greet Abraham. When he saw Abraham, a praise broke forth on his lips. He said (vv. 19,20):

> *Blessed be Abraham of the most high God, possessor of heaven and earth:*

The Blessing

> And blessed be the most high God, which hath delivered thine enemies into thy hand.

After this blessing, Abraham did a remarkable thing — something nobody had ever done before. Verse 20 says:

> And he gave him tithes of all.

Abraham gave "tithes of all" — not just a tithe of his money, but a tithe of *all* that he owned.

When Abraham saw that God literally possessed heaven and earth, and that He had delivered him from every enemy he confronted, Abraham reached into his life's possessions and gave tithes of everything.

We, who are of the faith of Abraham, need to come to know what Abraham knew as he gave those tithes and offerings to the Lord.

Abraham recognized the three most important things about God:

> The Lord is the most high God.
> He is the possessor of heaven and earth.
> He is the deliverer from all our enemies.

Abraham had believed in God, but he had not understood these three things about God. He had not realized how great his God was. Then, suddenly he had a revelation of it.

He could see God as his provider, the possessor of heaven and earth, the giver of *all* good things, the deliverer from all his enemies.

When Abraham saw Who his God really was, it caused him to give, to return his blessing to God.

Many people believe that tithing was instituted by the Mosaic Law, but Abraham gave these tithes to God over 400 years *before* Moses received the Law.

Tithing became a part of the Law of Moses through the understanding that they were to believe God as most high God, possessor of heaven and earth, and deliverer from all enemies. Because God was all these things to them, they gave tithes and offerings to Him. Tithing was a creative part of their overall faith in Who God was *and* who they were as God's people.

ABRAHAM'S BLESSING

The blessing that Melchizedek pronounced over Abraham is still in effect today. That blessing is for

The Blessing

us now because we are the seed of Abraham. We can accept that blessing and see God just as Abraham saw Him at that moment.

After Abraham had given tithes of all, the King of Sodom approached him and pointed to all the loot. In verses 21-23, we read:

> And the king of Sodom said unto Abraham, Give me the persons, and take the goods to thyself.

> And Abraham said to the king of Sodom, I have lift up mine hand unto the Lord, the most high God, the possessor of heaven and earth,

> That I will not take from a thread even to a shoelatchet, and that I will not take any thing that is thine, lest thou shouldest say, I have made Abraham rich.

I want you to pay close attention to Abraham's response to the offer of the King of Sodom. Most Christians have never really grasped what is being said. Let's read it again:

> I have lift up mine hand unto the Lord, the most high God, the possessor of heaven and earth,

Flood Tide

> That I will not take from a thread even to a shoelatchet, and that I will not take any thing that is thine, lest thou shouldest say, I have made Abraham rich.

Abraham gave tithes of all and put his complete trust only in God. With his hand raised to God, his Source, Abraham refused to accept anything from that man. He declared to the King of Sodom: "God will make me rich, not you!"

Some Christians today will accept money from anyone. But not Abraham! He knew Who his God was! And he knew his tithes were *seed* from which God would bless him and supply all his needs.

Abraham gave tithes of *everything*. Then when he was old and ready to die, it is written of him:

> And Abraham was old, and well stricken in age: and the Lord had blessed Abraham in all things.

> Genesis 24:1

Abraham's *seed-faith* had really worked in his life. Can you say, "I am blessed in *all* things. I am blessed in *everything*"?

The Blessing

Do you even believe it is possible?

It was possible with Abraham, but not by accident. God had blessed him in *all* things because Abraham recognized Who God was. Then he recognized who he was and gave his tithes as seed to God.

If you do not know Who God is, you will never know who *you* are. And you will never give your tithes to the Lord as Abraham did.

The King of Sodom tried to buy him off, but Abraham refused adamantly, saying:

"My God is most high. He owns everything! My God owns it all!

"Why should I stoop to take even a shoelace? Then you could brag and say, 'Look what I did for Abraham!'

"No, king, my God will make me rich. You're no source to me. My God is my *Source!*

"My God is higher than you. He is higher than your god. Your god couldn't even keep you from being captured.

"My God not only kept me from being captured, He gave me power to rescue you. He gave me power to rescue your people. He gave me power to rescue my nephew and his family, and to bring back all that was taken.

"My God delivered me from all my enemies. He is most high. He owns it all; and because I worship and give tithes to Him as my Source, He will make me richer than you can. It is God Who gives power to get wealth because only God owns the wealth of the world."

3
God's Chosen People

"And I will make my covenant between me and thee, and will multiply thee exceedingly."
                                            Genesis 17:2

Chapter 3
God's Chosen People

Abraham believed God. He became a man of faith, the miracle-working kind of faith that enabled him to *live* the fullest life of all.

Abraham was a hundred years old and Sarah, his wife, was ninety when God spoke to him and told him that they would bear a child.

Abraham believed what God told him. He believed this incredible promise because his worship of God and his giving tithes to God were in the rhythm of faith. His *seed-faith* was being constantly planted to God.

Miraculously, Sarah conceived and bore a son, Isaac.

That miracle birth was the beginning of the people who would come to be known through the world as "God's Chosen People." People who, as children of Abraham, believed God was the most high God, possessor of heaven and earth, deliverer from all their enemies, and multiplier of their tithes given to Him to meet their needs.

BIRTH OF A NATION

Abraham begat Isaac, the "son of promise."

Isaac begat Jacob. (Jacob's name was later changed to Israel because he chose to stop living by his wits and start trusting God as his *Source*.)

Jacob, or Israel, bore twelve sons whose descendants came to be known as "the twelve tribes of Israel." Their descendants became the children of Israel, and from them came our Savior, Jesus Christ, Whom St. Paul calls "the Son of David." (Rom. 1:3.) Notice that the *seed-faith* principle brought our Savior Jesus into the world.

The nation of Israel was established by God. They were the one people who were chosen by God. Though the world hated them, it had to respect them and say, "They are the most delightful people, the most delightsome land" (Mal. 3:12).

As these people of God obeyed the Lord, having the faith of Abraham to believe God as he did, and to give as he did, God's righteousness covered them.

God's Chosen People

When God looked at them, He looked at His own righteousness, for that is what their faith reflected.

It is very important that you understand these things:

- The descendants of Abraham, in becoming a nation and living in the faith of their father Abraham, understood Who God was.

- They understood that God is the most high God, the possessor of heaven and earth, and the deliverer from their enemies.

- In knowing their God as the Source of their total supply, they reached the place that they joyously gave tithes of all they had. And God's blessings were on them exactly as they were upon Abraham. He *blessed* them and *made* them a *blessing*.

- They were so prosperous, so blessed, so anointed of God that they conquered everything before them. As long as they looked to God as their Source, they could not be defeated. In being *blessed* they were made a *blessing* to all people.

BUT THEY TURNED AWAY

The children of Israel were the most victorious people in the history of the world!

Flood Tide

But they made a fatal mistake, and you must understand what this mistake was: They turned from their faith and, therefore, away from the most high God.

As individuals and as a nation who were God's people, they forgot Who God was. When they forgot Who God was, then they no longer knew who they were.

At that point in their lives, they *stopped* giving their tithes and offerings which God could bless and multiply for their full supply.

They began to think of other gods and their greatest sin became idol worship. They made gods with their hands and put them on high hills. They worshipped the works of their hands.

They put these other gods before the most high God and reduced the most high God to the lowest rank of gods.

Without God as their *Source* and without combining their worship of God with their giving, these once-prosperous, once-successful, once-spiritual people began to create their own gods. Living no longer in the faith of Abraham, their disobedience and sin against God brought them poverty and captivity.

God's Chosen People

Their enemies overcame them. Far from God, they lost their joy, they lost their song, they lost the meaning of their lives.

DELIVERED FROM BONDAGE

One of the most powerful things we can say about the Israelites' time of bondage in Egypt is that the Egyptian diseases did not come on them.

Even though the children of Israel were slaves to the Egyptians and were reduced to the lowest class of living, there was no sickness among them.

God said, *I will put none of the diseases of Egypt upon you*, and not a disease of Egypt came upon their bodies! (Ex.15:26.)

They were placed into the hands of their enemies. But according to Abraham and his faith, God was the deliverer from all their enemies.

Again recognizing the God of Abraham as their deliverer, they cried out to Him: "Deliver us from our enemies!"

God heard their cry.

He raised up the man Moses to lead His people out of bondage. As God's deliverer, Moses stood before Pharaoh and, in the name of the Lord, said, "Let My people go!"

And with the faith of Moses working mighty miracles, Pharaoh had no choice but to give in to the command of God to free His people.

A JOURNEY OF MIRACLES

When the children of Israel left Egypt, it was in the power of their faith, and they entered into a continuous stream of miracles.

They crossed the Red Sea as on dry land and journeyed through the desert to the "Land of Promise," the land God had given Abraham because of his faith and obedience.

The children of Israel overcame sickness. They were no longer poor. They were people of plenty!

Every financial need was met.

Every food need was met.

Their clothes lasted longer than ordinary.

They entered the Promised Land with the shout of a king!

Joshua, Moses' successor, was told by God to meditate in the Word of the Lord day and night. God said if he would believe and be obedient to these instructions, he would prosper and have good success. (Josh. 1:8.)

CAPTIVE AGAIN

But the children of Israel had the God-given power of choice. Joshua called upon them to *choose this day whom ye will serve* (Josh. 24:15).

And again they chose to *stop* believing God as most high God and, therefore, again stopped giving tithes and offerings. As a result, they did not let God be God to them. They believed they could make it without trusting in God and obeying Him.

Without God as Source and Deliverer, they were invaded by enemy armies. The Assyrians came in and captured ten of the twelve tribes of Israel. Those ten have not been found to this day.

The two remaining tribes — Judah and Benjamin — who controlled Jerusalem and the Temple were invaded by King Nebuchadnezzar of Babylon.

The walls of the City of God were torn down and His Temple was destroyed.

The people of Israel were captured and taken to faraway Babylon, a city which worshipped

Flood Tide

Nebuchadnezzar as god. When they went into captivity, they couldn't even sing. They had lost their song. The music and the joy of the Lord in their hearts were gone.

After seventy years, a remnant of the Israelites were permitted to return to their homeland. Only a handful of men — like Nehemiah, Ezra, Malachi, and Haggai — held on to their faith and understood that it was by faith in the most high God that it was made possible for them to come out of Babylonian captivity and return home.

Nehemiah rallied the people to believe God, to rebuild the walls of the city and restore the Temple. But many chose to put God down. When they returned to Jerusalem, they began to build fine houses for themselves. They did not provide for the House of God.

When they built only for themselves and failed to give to God, they cut themselves off from their *Source*. They cut themselves off from the most high God, possessor of heaven and earth, deliverer from all their enemies, and multiplier of their seed-faith.

While the prophets of God — Nehemiah, Ezra, Haggai, and Malachi — called upon them to reconnect their lives with God, they felt no need of God.

God's Chosen People

When water is cut off at its source, you cannot get water.

The same is true with God.

When you cut yourself off from Him, you cannot receive from Him.

You will not know Who God is, nor will you be able to receive what God has.

And that is exactly what happened to the children of Israel, even after God had brought them back to Jerusalem, to the House of God and His ways. They were no longer in *relationship* with Him to receive His blessings.

4
"Return Unto Me"

"Return unto me, and I will return unto you, saith the Lord of hosts."

Malachi 3:7

Chapter 4
"Return Unto Me"

The prophet Malachi was the last spokesman of the most high God to the children of Israel. His writings are recorded in the final book of the Old Testament.

In the first chapter, we find God making His final plea to the nation of Israel through the prophet Malachi. What began so many years before with faithful Abraham is now coming to a crashing conclusion.

GOD'S LOVE FOR HIS PEOPLE

Malachi has a burden. He begins his writing in chapter 1 with these words:

> *The burden of the word of the Lord to Israel by Malachi.*

Flood Tide

Then in verse 2 he quotes God: *I have loved you, saith the Lord.*

In the New Testament in 1 John 4:8 we are told *God is love.* But St. John is only re-stating an everlasting truth. God had always been love because love is His nature. Malachi begins his final plea with God saying, *I have loved you.*

When you think of how often you and I go astray, and yet God keeps on loving us, it should bring us to our knees crying, *God, I'm not worthy. But thank You for loving me.*

God was telling His people again: *I have loved you.*

Yet they ask, "Wherein have You loved us?" (v. 2.)

So God began to recount the ways. He reminded them how He had picked them up in Egypt and brought them out with a high hand to the land of their father Abraham.

They had come out of the loins of Abraham and had taken hold of Abraham's faith.

They had proclaimed the Lord as the most high God.

They had recognized the Lord God as owner of the heavens and the earth.

They saw God as their Source, and they knew they would lack nothing.

They had seen God deliver them from all their enemies — spiritual, physical, and financial.

God had blessed them.

He had made them the head and not the tail.

He looked at them through His own righteousness.

They were the apple of His eye.

BUT AGAIN THEY FAILED TO OBEY

In the second chapter of Malachi, God calls His people to task because of their disobedience and failure to follow in the steps of Abraham's faith. In verses 2,3 He says to them:

> *If ye will not hear, and if ye will not lay it to heart, to give glory unto my name, saith the Lord of hosts* (that means the Lord and His angels), *I will even send a curse upon you, and I will curse your*

Flood Tide

blessings: yea, I have cursed them already, because ye do not lay it to heart.

Behold, I will corrupt your seed, and spread dung upon your faces, even the dung of your solemn feasts; and one shall take you away with it.

These are harsh words, but God was angry with His people for choosing to cut themselves off from the faith of Abraham . . . and from *Him* Who was their only *Source!* He was angry because they were destroying themselves. The most terrible destruction to God is man's destruction of Himself by going away from his *Source.*

GOD'S FINAL PLEA

In the third chapter of Malachi, God makes a final effort to bring the children of Israel back to the faith of Abraham — the faith that you and I have today by being "in Christ."

Let's read beginning with verse 7:

Even from the days of your fathers ye are gone away from mine ordinances, and have not kept them. Return unto me,

"Return Unto Me"

and I will return unto you, saith the Lord of hosts.

When God says, Return unto me, He is talking about Who He is, not what this world thinks He is. You see, God did not leave the children of Israel; they left Him.

This is what the Lord is saying:

Return unto Me, the most high God.

Return unto Me, the possessor of heaven and earth.

Return unto Me, the deliverer from all your enemies.

The Lord was saying:

"Return unto Me! Come back to Me! Leave the false gods you created by the works of your hands. They are nothing.

"Turn away from thinking you control the heavens and the earth. You don't!

"Turn away from trusting in earthly powers to deliver you. They can't!

"Come back to Me. I can deliver you from all your enemies."

The children of Israel had forgotten their *Source*.

They had not acknowledged receiving their blessings from the God Who is most high, but had taken them from the heavens and the earth without a right. They had let man and earthly things become their source. Unlike Abraham who would not allow anyone but God to make him rich, they tried to get rich through man only.

Haggai 2:8 states that the Lord owns all the silver and gold in the earth, so we could read Malachi 3:7 this way:

"I, God, owner of all the silver and gold in the earth, will return unto you."

How would you like for the One Who owns all the silver and gold to return to you? I pray we will learn Who really owns the silver and the gold, and get it straight in our thinking that when we make Him God of our lives, we also make Him the Source of our total supply.

"Return Unto Me"

GOD IS ROBBED

Again, in Malachi 3:7 God says, *Return unto me, and I will return unto you, saith the Lord of hosts. But ye said, Wherein shall we return?*

God has said, "Come back to Me, and I will come back to you."

But they say, "What do You mean, 'Return to You'? We haven't even left You." (It's bad enough to leave God by failing to use your faith, but it's even worse not to know you are gone!)

God answers their question by asking a question: *Will a man rob God? Yet ye have robbed me* (v. 8).

Then they ask, *Wherein have we robbed thee?* (v. 8).

God's answer: *In tithes and offerings.*

How could anybody rob God?

Is it possible for God to be robbed?

Yes!

This is one of the fatalistic moments in our lives:

when we go so far from remembering Who God is and who we are until we become robbers of God.

It is bad to rob the creatures on God's earth. But how bad is it to rob God?

The worst thief in the world is the one who robs God in tithes and offerings.

To rob God is to put ourselves out of harmony with the heavens and the earth — the supernatural and natural coming together for our total supply.

To rob God is to turn away from the only Deliverer we can know. When we turn away from Him, we have turned away from our *Source*.

When thieves are put in jail; that jail with iron bars is bad, but it is really the least of their imprisonment. The real imprisonment is their separation from God. They are isolated with other people who also are separated from God. In a jail or prison, criminals are isolated from other people and put together in cells — criminal with criminal.

That is what these people were before God: "You are isolated from Me. You are now together with other people who are isolated from Me. Worst of all, you have robbed Me! You are robbers and

"Return Unto Me"

thieves. Therefore, you are in jail — spiritually, physically, financially!"

Who did they rob?

The most high God — possessor of heaven and earth, deliverer from all their enemies, the Name that is above every name.

God is saying, "Is it possible that you would rob the most high God, the God Who owns all the silver and gold? Would you be that stupid? Would you rob the One Who has it all? You have robbed Me."

But ye say, Wherein have we robbed thee?

They had gone so far away from God that they did not even know they had robbed Him. They had forgotten Him to the extent that they did not even know they had done it. Their *relationship* with God was gone!

They ask, Wherein have we robbed thee?

God replies, In *tithes and offerings.*

When Abraham recognized God as the most high God, possessor of heaven and earth, deliverer from all his enemies, what did he do? He gave tithes of *all,* of *everything!*

God's financial system for His work and our needs was instituted at that moment; then it was passed down through the children of Israel. Because of Who God was and who they were, they were to give tithes of all as their *firstfruits*. This became their *seed-faith*. This is how God's beautiful "giving and receiving" system started! This was when seedtime and harvest went into effect.

The children of Israel had been worshipping God and giving Him all their tithes and offerings; but in Malachi's day, they had strayed so far from God that they no longer recognized Who He was. Having lost their *relationship*, they did not know they had been robbing God and they did not know what they had robbed Him of.

I want you to notice that God said this in *love*. He was not beating them over the head; He was telling them the truth: "You have robbed Me; and you ask how? In tithes and offerings."

In verse 9, the Lord continues by saying, *Ye are cursed with a curse: for ye have robbed me, even this whole nation.*

Notice He did not say, "I am going to curse you."

"Return Unto Me"

The curse which came upon them was actually self-inflicted. They thought they knew God, but they really did not know Him at all.

They were withholding from the God Who is most high, the possessor of heaven and earth, the deliverer from all their enemies. To withhold from Him the very thing He is going to multiply and bless is just like withholding seed from your garden.

The withholding of seed will bring a curse on the garden.

If a wheat farmer does not plant wheat seed, his fields will be cursed from the lack of seed to grow. How can anything grow when there is nothing planted? Zero multiplied is still zero!

This is what God was saying: *Ye are cursed with a curse: for ye have robbed me, even this whole nation.*

"PROVE ME . . ."

Then God appeals to the nation of Israel in verse 10:

> *Bring ye all the tithes into the storehouse, that there may be meat in mine house.*

Flood Tide

Bring ye . . . Who is *ye*? That's you and me who are "sons and daughters of Abraham." Who else is going to bring tithes and offerings if we don't?

. . . that there may be meat in mine house. The word *meat* means "resources."

So God is saying to His people: "Here is what I want you to do: Bring all your tithes and offerings into My storehouse and there will be resources in My house."

Please realize this: God does not need our tithes and offerings. He is not hungry or without raiment. He does not want our money for Himself. He wants it for only one reason: so there will be resources available among His people — resources from which they can draw *according to His riches.* (Phil 4:19.)

Bring ye all the tithes into the storehouse, that there may be meat in mine house, and prove me now herewith, saith the Lord of hosts, if I will not open you the windows of heaven, and pour you out a blessing, that there shall not be room enough to receive it.

"Return Unto Me"

NO LACK WITH GOD

God is saying:

"You bring in your tithes and offerings. Then I will have a storehouse of resources from which you can draw your supply.

"In addition to that, I will open the windows of heaven which you have shut up against yourself. I will walk in, take your disobedience, and fling it aside.

"Then I will roll open the windows of heaven and pour through them upon you a blessing that you will not have room enough to contain. You will get so much that you will not even know what to do with it!

"I will give to you from what I own, and I own the heavens and the earth."

All the gold God ever put in this earth is still here today. Not one ounce of that gold has disappeared. With God, there is no poverty, no recession, no depression, no want, no lack.

All the blessing and multiplying power of God for our seed sown is still here. In Galatians 6:7-9 God says: "You *sow* it, I will *grow* it; and you will *reap* it . . . all in *due season*."

Flood Tide

Isn't it time you and I wake up from our long sleep and get into a relationship with the most high God that we might be *blessed* and made a *blessing*?

5
God Is Our Deliverer

"The silver is mine, and the gold is mine, saith the Lord of hosts."
Haggai 2:8

Chapter 5
God Is Our Deliverer

Some people think that all you need to do is get saved and give your heart to the Lord, then you will go to heaven. This is true, but you can live a long time before you will go to heaven.

I was converted when I was seventeen years old, and I have had to live in this body on this earth ever since. I have had to provide food and clothing for my body, a house over my head, a car to drive, and money to pay bills. I have faced the same situations in my life that you have faced.

It is true that God is very concerned about whether or not we go to heaven; but He is also very concerned about us while we are living on this earth. In the Lord's prayer, He teaches us to pray: *Thy will be done in earth as it is in heaven.*

Flood Tide

Many people get saved, then turn away from the Lord later in life because all they have been taught is that they are going to heaven. Of course, all of us want to go to heaven, but we have to live this life first.

Some of the most miserable people I have ever known are Christians who don't trust God as their Source here on earth.

I receive thousands of letters from both Christians and sinners. Some of the most pathetic ones are from people who believe they are serving the Lord. Yet so much is missing in their lives because they are robbing God of the very thing — their seed-faith giving — which He uses to multiply back in blessings of supply to them.

The world needs to see Christians with the glory of the Lord shining on their faces, with a shout in their souls and victory in their lives . . . because they are releasing their faith to God and He is meeting need after need in their lives.

As Christians, we should be living our lives on earth with the sure knowledge and faith that God wishes *above all things* that we *prosper and be in health,* even as our souls prosper. (3 John 2.) We can accept God's highest wish for us and practice the

God Is Our Deliverer

seed-faith life for God to help us support ourselves, our families, and His great work on earth.

But most Christians are not enjoying God's highest wish for them spiritually, physically, or financially. Furthermore, they don't even think that they can... or should! So they are merely *existing* on earth in a self-defeating life.

Listen, my friend, God is not raining money out of heaven. All the money we need is right here in the earth. But we must recognize that God is our Source. Then you can understand God saying, *Return unto me.*

If we do not return to our God and know Who He is and how He works in us on earth, He will not return to us.

Remember: In Haggai 2:8, God tells us that all the silver and gold of the earth are His. But that is hard to believe when you go out into the world and look around.

It appears that wicked people have control of that wealth. Last year alone, we are told $60 billion was spent on liquor! Just think what God's people could do with that same amount of money.

It is a crime not to live in *seed-faith* and let the devil's crowd have control of the wealth of God's earth!

Do you ever think about getting mad at the devil? I do! He has robbed God's people of the wealth in the earth — the silver and gold that God put here for them! He has also robbed them of believing that good medical care is for them. He has robbed them of believing God heals through prayer. And he has robbed them only because they have let him do it!

The devil thinks he owns it all. He even tried to offer it to Jesus if Jesus would worship him. But Jesus knew it wasn't the devil's to offer and that it is the Lord God only that we are to worship. Jesus knew there was a fuller and greater prosperity in serving God than in going into business with the devil.

All our health is not coming miraculously. Much of our health is potentially from several areas: our own body's healing properties, the chemicals of God's earth which He enables skilled physicians to administer, the proper exercising of our bodies, the right thinking and believing of our minds, and the prayers of faith available to us here on earth. Again we must recognize that God is our Source of the natural.

God Is Our Deliverer

Also, all our spiritual help does not flow out of heaven. God has put His churches here on earth and has promised that where two or three are gathered together in His name, "I am in the midst of them." (Matt. 18:20.)

Do you know where the word *prosperity* came from? It came from God!

Do you know where the word *success* came from? It came from God!

I believe my God is the most high God, owner of heaven and earth, deliverer from all my enemies. I believe God fully intends for His people to be prosperous and have good success. But I believe they can be neither prosperous nor successful as long as they do not know who or what their position is before God.

The world today is ruled by the prince of the power of the air — the devil; the thief who, as Jesus said, came to steal, to kill, and to destroy. (John 10:10.) This world has followed the devil, and he has rewarded their loyalty by stealing from them every ounce of the kind of prosperity and success they might possess.

Flood Tide

The devil has stolen the prosperity and success that God's people should be enjoying to the fullest, and only because we allow him to do it.

The people who make up this world do not believe that God is the most high God, the possessor of the heavens and the earth. They think they possess it, just as the world's people did in Abraham's day.

Abraham's world and our world do not believe that God is the deliverer from all their enemies. They think they can do it; but if they can, they would be doing a much better job of it.

People run around trying to meet important people. They would give anything if they could just shake the hand of a V.I.P.!

They think the names of certain people are above other names. I respect the President of the United States, but his name is not above the name of our Savior. Nobody's name is above the name of Jesus!

St. Paul tells us in Ephesians 1:20-22 and Philippians 2:6-11 that God has given Jesus a name that is above every name . . . and above everything that is named in this world. Also, he says that all things have been put under Jesus' feet. All things! You name it!

God Is Our Deliverer

Sin? Jesus' name is above it!

Fear? Jesus' name is above it!

Cancer? Jesus' name is above it, as well as all other diseases!

Financial need? Jesus' name is above it!

We have allowed the devil to steal from us because we have forgotten Who our God is and who we are, and therefore have failed to give our tithes as seed-faith to Him.

People who do not know Who God is are without *identity*. They do not know who or what they are, and they can be neither prosperous nor successful in the ways God has provided for them. They allow themselves to be defeated by the devil and stay tormented throughout their lives.

It is by knowing God and knowing Who He is that shows you who you are.

When you know God, you become somebody. You take on the identity of God, your Father; Jesus Christ, your Savior; the Holy Spirit, your Comforter; the children of God, your brothers and sisters; and heaven, your eternal home.

Flood Tide

The new understanding that the Holy Spirit *indwells* us and enables us to pray both *with the spirit* (in tongues), *and with the understanding* (1 Cor. 14:15) is bringing us back to that intimate knowledge of knowing Who God is.

This helps us realize again that God is the most high God. To see that our God and His heirs (that's us!) own the heavens and the earth.

Once we know we are in God, we can know how He commands the right things for us. He commands this earth to give up its riches. He commands the windows of heaven to open up to us. But we must choose to believe it so that when we give, we open ourselves up to *receive*.

God moves in our midst to deliver us from our enemies. To set us free! To make us whole! He is our God! He is our Deliverer from sin, demons, fear, sickness, financial need — and from making this world our source.

As God moves among us in limitless power, we must understand Who He is, and who we are, in order to trust Him as our Source of total supply. Long ago Abraham released his faith to do this, the first man to actually do it. As his sons and daughters in the faith of Jesus Christ, our privileges are equal to

His and even above His through the name of Jesus Christ and the New Covenant He purchased for us through His shed blood at Calvary.

BEHIND THE CROSS

Let me illustrate this with a word about the Cross. Some Christians have never heard that they can go behind the Cross. They have only heard about Jesus being nailed to it. They visualize Him hanging there with the nails in His hands and feet.

They stand in front of the Cross and look up at His blood being shed. But is has never occurred to them that they can also go behind the Cross.

Behind the Cross, you will find His back where He was whipped for you. They put stripes on His back for *your* healing.

The blood coming from those stripes on His back is for our healing.

Most Christians have never stepped behind the Cross for their full health. They only stand in front of it for their soul's salvation.

We need to walk in a *circle* around the Cross. While in front of it, we receive His sacrifice for our sins being washed away. While behind it, we accept healing for our bodies.

Lay claim to what is yours.

Lay claim to it by your *seed-faith*, then speak to the mountain in your life and tell it to go! In Matthew 17:20 Jesus says when you make your faith as a seed you sow, then you are to *speak* to your mountain of need. Tell it to be removed. The mountain will obey you and be removed! Then Jesus says, *And nothing shall be impossible unto you.*

Abraham did this and God "gave him everything." Abraham looked through the ages with his faith and saw Jesus. Before Jesus was ever born, before He went to the cross for our sins and rose from the dead for our salvation, before He ascended back to heaven and sent the Holy Spirit to *indwell* us forever, Abraham *saw* that Jesus' name was above every name, that He possessed it all, that He was the deliverer from all our enemies. Abraham saw that and he rejoiced!

Abraham *saw* all that *before*. You and I live *after* what Abraham saw before. He did not have the written Scriptures as we do. We have all Abraham had, plus the Christ Who has come *and* the living written Word of God to tell us about it so we can release our faith.

Therefore, it is high time to use the name of Jesus and command the devil to take his hands off God's property. That's you!

You have ministering angels (the heavenly hosts) whose purpose in the world is to minister *for* you. (Heb. 1:14.)

You can release your faith for Jesus to send your angel on a mission of deliverance on your behalf. Your angel can take from the devil's hand what the devil stole from you, then bring it back and put it in your hands again.

You need to open your spiritual eyes to what your God-appointed angel can do for you right here on earth.

6
Tithing In The Seed-Faith Way

"I am . . . thy exceeding
great reward."
            Genesis 15:1

6
Tithing In The Seed-Faith Way

The children of Israel came out of the loins of Abraham, the same as we Christians today by our faith in Jesus Christ are the sons and daughters of Abraham.

Abraham saw Jesus. He saw His day. Jesus said, "Abraham saw my day and he rejoiced." (John 8:56.)

Abraham looked by faith through the ages, hundreds of years before Christ was born, and actually saw Jesus with his spiritual eyes.

You need to study Abraham's life. Take time to read the 11th chapter of Hebrews. Time after time, you will find the phrase: "Abraham by faith . . . Abraham by faith . . . Abraham by faith . . ."

Flood Tide

Abraham was a seed-faith man. He was our example as a seed-faith man. We began to get into seed-faith when we believed God to save us through Jesus Christ. Now we need to get into "daily" seed-faith like Abraham did. I assure you that we can.

We know how to get into fear by simply not using our faith to believe God. But what has fear ever done for anyone?

We know how to get into unbelief by holding back our faith. But what has unbelief ever done for anyone?

We can learn to get into faith as a seed we plant and *live* in seed-faith every day of our lives. But we will never live in seed-faith if we don't even know Who God is.

The children of Israel knew Who God was. God said to Abraham, "I know you will command your children after you." He taught his descendants to look upon God as the most high God, possessor of heaven and earth, deliverer from all their enemies, and to give tithes of all to Him.

Nobody in Israel was poor. There was not a poor person among them; but there were poor people that passed through from other lands. So the

Israelites did not harvest the corners of their fields. They left that part of their crop for the poor of other nations that were passing through.

Has it ever occurred to you why there were no poor people in Israel?

Because they knew Who their God was!

They knew He possessed the heavens and the earth. They knew He delivered them from their enemies.

As they gave the Lord their tithes and offerings — their firstfruits, the best that they had — they gave it as a seed, and the Lord blessed their crops. He blessed them so much that when they had finished harvesting, it was time to plant again. They couldn't get one harvest in until it was time to plant again!

This happened because these people had the faith of Abraham. They recognized Who God was; and, in knowing God, they knew who they were and gave God their best.

The Israelites who followed the faith of Abraham experienced personally and as a people God pouring upon them the *blessings* of Abraham.

What are "the blessings of Abraham"?

Hebrews 6:13,14 says:

> For when God made promise to Abraham, because he could swear by no greater, he sware by himself,
>
> Saying, Surely blessing I will bless thee, and multiplying I will multiply thee.

The Israelites were blessed and multiplied!

Some might say, "But that was a different age."

Yes, but it is still the same God! He is the same yesterday, today, and forever. (Heb. 13:8.)

It is the same faith. According to the New Testament, there is only one faith. (Eph. 4:5.)

The faith they had in that day is no different from the faith we have today. It is one faith, just like gold is gold. No matter when you find it, gold is still gold. Faith is faith in every age.

Am I saying that today on this earth we can do what God said and He will do what He said He would do?

Yes!

There is every scriptural reason that if anybody should prosper, it should be a child of God! If anybody should be blessed and multiplied, it should be Christians!

To receive what God has for us, we must *do* what God has said for us to *do*.

DON'T PAY, GIVE

Someone said, "I pay my tithes, but nothing ever happens to me."

Yes, I can understand that. Most Christians don't even know how God's tithing system started and what it was designed to do for God's people.

By the time of Jesus' birth, the children of Israel had been taken over by a certain type of religious leader. These leaders thought they were great tithers. They *paid* tithes, but they had ceased *giving* them in the spirit of the understanding Abraham had of knowing Who God was, and therefore who he was. These so-called religious leaders, who no longer knew Who God was and therefore who they were, missed God's system completely.

And, remember, these leaders lived in Jesus' day, but they didn't have the slightest idea that He was the One Abraham had seen by faith.

Flood Tide

They would take the seed that was to be planted in their fields and put aside an *exact* tenth as their tithe. They would produce thousands and thousands of seeds, but there would not be one extra grain given to the Lord. They went to great trouble to be exact and perfect in the measurement of what they gave to God.

They were unwilling givers. God was not really their God. They didn't know Him as a personal God to them.

There was no understanding that God's tithing system is based on faith . . . that it is a seed of faith . . . and that they were to expect to receive from God.

They did not give their tithes in the faith of Abraham and therefore did not qualify before God to be given the "blessing of Abraham."

They had ruled out God as owner of the heavens and the earth.

They had lost their sense of justice and mercy. They stooped so low that when they rented their houses to widows, they doubled and tripled the rent.

Their love and concern for people was gone from their hearts.

Tithing In The Seed-Faith Way

They had faith but used it to believe wrongly about Who God was and who they should be.

There is more to the blessings of God than *paying* tithes. If you think that all you have to do is *pay* your tithes and offerings to God, you are wrong.

First, you have to return to Him and all that He really is. *Then*, and only then, are you to *bring* in your tithes and offerings as seed sown unto God, your Source. You can't just bring in money and, as it were, throw it at God's feet, and say, "I've done it."

If we had all the money in the world, could we pay God?

No.

How can you pay for something that Jesus has already paid in full?

You can't *pay* God, but you can *give* to Him. You can plant seed unto the Lord and expect the return He has guaranteed to give to you.

God doesn't want your money without your heart. He wants you!

We can't build for God with money alone; we must have people. People are the builders. People make things run. Money alone can't get the job done. It will simply remain in a bank or a billfold until someone puts it to use. It is people who put money to its God-appointed use. It is God's people acting in faith and love who accomplish things.

Let's forget about *paying* and accept the cross of Jesus Christ as total payment.

Have you accepted the Cross — the crucified Christ?

Have you realized that Jesus Christ paid it all for you?

Quit trying to *pay* God. You can't pay Him anything.

Start *giving* your seed to Him for planting — not as a debt you owe, but as a seed you sow for God to grow and multiply for His work and for the supplying of all your need. Then you will get into the miracle of *seed-faith*!

He said, *Return unto me.*

You say that you are saved, but have you returned your life and the daily living of it to God? A newborn baby is helpless until it starts learning, growing, and becoming a mature person to live a whole life.

Sometimes getting saved is like a wasp — bigger when it is born that when it is full grown. Some Christians seem to have more when they first get saved than they have in their later years.

You return unto the most high God, possessor of heaven and earth, deliverer from all your enemies.

God said, "Return unto me, and I will return unto you."

The people answered, "But how shall we return unto You? If we've gone away from You, how shall we return?"

His answer was simple: *In tithes and offerings.*

Why did God say that? Because that was where the *final break* had come between them and Him.

TITHING WITH JOY

At the heart of their relationship with God was the fact that they had known Who God was and who they were. Secondly, they had given Him the firstfruits — their very best as their tithes and offerings — and they gave them with joy as seeds of their faith in the most high God.

It was a high day, a day of joy, when they took the firstfruits before the Lord. It was a celebration of their love and faith . . . and their expectation to be blessed.

Why?

Because the individual people of Israel knew their best seed had been planted — not just in the ground but in the Lord. They knew the Lord would give them blessings in return, the blessings of Abraham, "the father of all who have faith."

God said to Israel, *Blessing I will bless thee, and multiplying I will multiply thee.*

Therefore, the happiest day in Israel was when they brought in the firstfruits to give to God. But they quit bringing in their tithes and offerings. They quit because they stopped believing that God was the most high God, that He possessed everything, that He was the deliverer from all their enemies and the Source of their lives.

Why do people today fail to bring in their tithes and offerings, fail to give *seed-faith*? Because they do not believe that God is God.

People say, "But He saved me. I'm a member of a church. I'm going to heaven."

Maybe so, but you will not be a very good witness to anybody before you get to heaven. The failure to live the *seed-faith life* causes other people to fail to see the faith of Abraham working in us to move our mountains of need — spiritually, physically, financially.

You might say to a friend, "I want you to come to the Lord. I'm a Christian."

But he looks at you, sees you with your needs tormenting you, and asks, "Why would I want to come to your God? So I can be like you?"

Some will even ask you, "So I can be broke as most of you Christians are?"

Maybe the God you know is poor, but the God I serve owns the heavens and the earth!

I am absolutely convinced that when you know Who God is and then who you are, you will come into the knowing of faith that God wants you to live in a nice house and drive a nice car — *but* He wants you to serve Him with it. God wants to prosper you so that, when you get prosperous, you will honor Jesus with it.

Start thinking prosperity. Don't think poor.

What did Abraham say?

"God will make me rich!"

What would you do if God made you prosper?

The first thing you would do is get happy, knowing you could pay your bills. Then you would know God would use your prosperity as a blessing to others.

I urge you to lay claim to your riches as the faith man, Abraham, did — riches that God, your Source, has provided for you and to be used through you for His glory.

Command the devil to take his hands off what is yours, and do it in Jesus' name.

Believe God to dispatch the ministering spirits, the angels of God, to retrieve those riches out of the devil's hands and put them in your billfold and bank account as your miracle harvest.

Start planting some seed, *and plant it out of your need.*

Begin to give God His tithes and offerings as *seed-faith*. Do it because of Who He is, and who you are, and do it because you have a need to do it.

RECEIVING BY FAITH

Someone said, "If I lived by faith, I would never have anything, or amount to anything."

No, if you live by faith, you will prosper and succeed.

The Old Testament says, *The just shall live by . . . faith* (Hab. 2:4). In Romans 1:17 the Apostle Paul states it again: *The just shall live by faith.*

During the 16th century, a Catholic priest named Martin Luther traveled to Rome from his home in Wittenberg, Germany. While in prayer and meditation, he found this verse in Romans 1:17 and began struggling with the question of faith and works.

When he returned home, he nailed a number of writings to his church door. And the Protestant Reformation was born! It swept to America and, suddenly, there was another people who started living by faith in God.

Flood Tide

It takes faith — and you have faith — to believe that God will really take care of you. And He will! Just make these simple, basic decisions in your heart:

God is the most high God to you.

God gave Jesus a name above every name, both in this world and in the world to come, and He placed all things under His feet.

God shall supply all your need according to His riches in glory by Christ Jesus. (Phil. 4:19.)

God owns the heavens and the earth.

God was manifested to destroy the works of the devil in your life and in all people.

God will deliver you from the enemy's hands if you seed your faith for Him to do it.

Everything that Abraham believed, you can believe.

If you have faith in Jesus, you have the same kind of faith that Abraham had. Our faith as Christians goes back beyond Moses and the Law to Abraham!

Tithing In The Seed-Faith Way

And where are we today? In the best position of our lives!

We are not in this world alone. Nor are we slaves to its system and economy. Men and women throughout the country are preaching the Word of God so we will, by the "hearing of faith," start saying to our faith: "Faith, come up out of me and go to God. Faith, I release you that God may bless me and make me a blessing."

We are not living on an earth that has no relationship to God and to us who know God. It is not an earth we are not supposed to live on.

We are not an earth that has nothing of value in it. The value God has put in His earth could feed billions of people without anyone going hungry or not having their needs met.

Everything in this earth belongs to God and to His children who live by faith. In the rhythm of our *seed-faith*, we can walk on this earth and say, "It is my God's; therefore, it is mine!"

None of the gold has been taken away. Everything is based on the gold standard. When you hear that the economy is going down, it is a lie! Man is missing God and manipulating things without Him as their Source!

God's economy never goes down! It is based on gold and all the gold He ever put here is still in the earth. It is here!

How do we get to it?

We don't. We get into position for God to get it for us!

By our seed-faith and honest work, He sends it to us.

I remember receiving a check from a man who didn't even like me. He said, "I'm sending you this check, but don't think I'm sending it because I like Oral Roberts. I wouldn't walk across the street to hear you preach. If you wonder why I'm sending it, even though I don't like you, it's because God told me to."

That man couldn't help himself. He had to obey God and send the check. And it cashed — all of it! I spent every dollar of it for the glory of God!

When you live in "giving first," as Jesus said in Luke 6:38, then men will give to you *good measure, pressed down, shaken together, and running over.* It's the "running over" that God has ordained for you to have.

Tithing In The Seed-Faith Way

TITHING BY FAITH

You say then, "How do I give tithes?"

You don't start by giving tithes. You start by asking yourself, "Who is God to me?"

Abraham said He is the most high God.

Paul said that Jesus' name is above every name that is named in this world and the world to come *and* that everything is under His feet.

Everything that is named is under Jesus' feet! Sin, disease, poverty, lack, enemies — all these things are under Jesus' feet.

And the Bible says He will supply all our needs according to *what*?

His poverty? No.

His riches by Christ Jesus in glory? Yes.

And He will deliver us from *whom*?

Our enemies!

He will make us prosperous. It is not your job or

business that makes you prosperous. God makes you prosperous *through* it, and in other ways, too. He is your *Source.*

"What if I lose my job? . . . my pension?"

If you don't lose God, you can lose all these and still get your need met. Why? Because God, your Source, will simply open a new door for you (or an old one), and let you discover even more than you lost!

When you give tithes of all, you are giving your faith; therefore, it is a seed you plant.

You are giving your love.

You are giving your justice.

You are giving your recognition of Who God is to you and who you are.

When you bring your tithes and offerings to the Lord, you are bringing your whole belief in God in the form of faith-seeds.

If you are just giving money, it won't work. God does not need your money; He needs *you!*

Tithing In The Seed-Faith Way

Why do you think He needs your money when He has all the gold and silver in the earth, as well as all the riches in glory by Christ Jesus?

Do you think He needs *your* money or *mine*?

No. He needs *you*, and He needs *me*.

He said, "You return unto Me. Bring in all the tithes and offerings. Prove Me now, and I will give you the evidence."

7
Flood Tide

"Prove me now . . .
I will . . . open you the windows of heaven,
and pour you out a blessing . . ."

                                      Malachi 3:10

Chapter 7
Flood Tide

> *Bring ye all the tithes into the storehouse, that there may be meat (or resources) in mine house, and prove me now . . .*
>
> Malachi 3:10

This is the only place in the Bible where God has said for us to prove Him.

He says, "Prove Me. Put Me to the test."

One man told me he was afraid to put God to the test, so I asked him why.

He answered, "What if He doesn't come through? Then I won't have any faith in Him."

I felt like saying, "Brother, you don't have any faith in Him now."

Why would God say to prove Him?

The answer is so simple that it can slip by us.

EVIDENCE

When you go into a court of law, the judge demands *evidence*.

When you order a piece of merchandise, you want *evidence* that it is what the seller says it is.

What is "the evidence"?

If I asked you to sit in a chair, you wouldn't consciously consider whether or not the chair could hold you. In your mind you would have "the evidence" that it will not collapse. You wouldn't sit in a chair that you knew would collapse and cause injury to your body.

FAITH IS THE EVIDENCE

Faith is based on evidence. Hebrews 11:1 says, *Now faith is the substance of things hoped for, the evidence of things not seen.*

How can you have *evidence* of things you cannot see?

This is where your faith comes in. You have to put your faith to work to find the *evidence* for what you cannot see.

We cannot see the air, but we have the evidence of it because we breathe it into our lungs.

What about gravity? We cannot see it or feel it, but we know it is there. Our ability to walk on the earth is the evidence of it.

God said, *Prove me now herewith.*

God has to be absolutely confident of Who He is to say, "Prove Me."

He is saying, "I will stand before you and let you put Me to the test. I am not going to tell you to prove Me unless I am provable, and I know that I am. I am not going to tell you to test Me unless I know that I will stand up to that test."

WINDOWS OF HEAVEN

God said:

> *Prove me now herewith, saith the Lord of hosts, if I will not open you the*

windows of heaven, and pour you out a blessing (not a curse, but a blessing!), that there shall not be room enough to receive it.

I want you to see this as God speaking to you personally. He is saying to you:

"You bring all your tithes into My storehouse so that there is meat (resources) in My house, and prove Me.

"I will do it for you: I will fling open the windows of heaven to you. Through them, I will pour out blessings upon you — so much so that there will not be room enough for you to contain it all!"

How would you like to be blessed so much that you couldn't carry it off, store it up, or contain it?

A FLOOD OF BLESSINGS

Notice, God said He would *pour* out a blessing on you. Think of a rain — a heavy rain, a downpour.

God said, "I will open the windows of heaven, and I will pour you out a blessing."

Have you ever thought how it would be for God to pour something?

Flood Tide

Picture in your mind God pouring. It would be a flood! Otherwise it could be contained, right? Remember, God said there will not be room enough to contain it. So it would have to be a flood.

What happened when God opened the windows of heaven in Genesis 7:11?

A flood came!

> And it came to pass after seven days, that the waters of the flood were upon the earth.

> In the six hundredth year of Noah's life, in the second month, the seventeenth day of the month, the same day were all the fountains of the great deep broken up, and the windows of heaven were opened (vv. 10,11).

The windows of heaven were opened!

It rained forty days and forty nights, so much that the earth could not contain it. The waters completely overflowed the earth.

God opened the windows of heaven and the rain came down. There was an abundance of water, and the earth could not contain it.

That is the kind of blessing God says He will give His people . . . give *you* . . . give *me*.

He said He Himself would open the windows of heaven and pour us out a blessing that there would not be room enough to contain it.

I want you to picture in your mind how great a blessing that really is. Think of a flood of blessing pouring forth from heaven. It would be more than you could contain by capacities you have.

God is talking about a *flood of blessings*. He is talking according to His nature.

What is God's nature? It is abundance.

When God blesses you, you are blessed as never before.

MUCH MORE THAN A TRICKLE

God didn't say, "I'll open the windows of heaven and pour you out a *trickle!*"

He didn't say, "I'll open the windows of heaven and pour you out a *stream!*"

He didn't say, "I'll open the windows of heaven and pour you out a *river!*"

Flood Tide

God said, "I'll open the windows of heaven and pour you out *a flood!*"

Some people are experiencing a trickle of God's blessings.

Some are in a stream of His blessings.

Others are trying to get into a river of His blessings.

But how many are in that flood stage?

I know everyone would like to be there, but how many are actually living there now?

If God's blessings are not overflowing you, you are not in the flood yet. Plant your seed out of your need and open yourself to receive. Watch for God to pour down His blessings on you until they are running over in your life.

I'm a candidate for the flood!

I want to go on through the trickle and through the stream. I want to get in the river just long enough to cross over and reach the flood. I want in that flood! I want in on those blessings that run over! I want in the flood stage!

Can you contain what God can do?

Flood Tide

Is there anybody in the world who can contain it?

No! God is too big!

When He pours out His blessings, it is impossible for us to contain it!

You can contain a trickle of water. Just get a bucket.

You can contain a stream or a river. Build a dam and the flow of water will be stopped.

But there is no way that you can contain a flood!

That is what your God wants to do for you. He wants to give you a flood of blessings!

In a recent seminar I conducted at Oral Roberts University with about 2200 people present, I asked how many were in that flood stage of God's blessings and were unable to contain the blessing that God had poured out upon them. Eight people stood up. Out of 2200 Christians, only 8 were in the flood stage.

I asked how many were in the river stage. About 50 stood up.

Flood Tide

When I asked how many were in the stream stage, about 200 stood up.

But when I asked how many were in the trickle stage, almost 2000 people stood up!

No wonder they were in the trickle stage: They had not yet understood Who God was. They were not giving tithes of all as their *seed-faith* to God like Abraham did, and they were not receiving the blessings of Abraham.

In that seminar we began to learn Who God was: that He is the most high God, possessor of heaven and earth, deliverer from all our enemies. When the people realized this, they saw the importance of making God their Source, of planting their seeds of faith for God to grow and multiply from His abundance, then to expect to receive from God's system of multiplication.

They wanted in on the flood tide of God's blessings! No wonder so many keep coming to these seminars. As they absorb God's holy Word on living in the rhythm of the *seed-faith life,* and start releasing their faith for their miracle harvests, they begin to enter flood stage. These dear seed-faith partners are the happiest people I have ever known. It's a joy to be around them.

Flood Tide

YOU CAN RECEIVE!

How do you receive more than just a trickle?

Return to God and honor Him as the most high God, Who has given His Son Jesus Christ a name above every name and put all things under His feet.

Recognize Him as the possessor of heaven *and* earth, owning all the gold and silver, all the chemicals for our better health, and all the fruit-bearing properties of earth and space. He said He will supply all your need according to *His* riches, not man's. That means from *both* heaven and earth.

Worship Him as Savior, Lord, and King with *all* your tithes and offerings. Not just one tithe, but *all* of them. Not just one offering, but *all* of them. Not just one time, but *all* the time! Not just your seed, but your *best* seed!

Do it regularly, rhythmically, expectantly. Make it your life's system because it is God's system, His only system.

Prove your God. He will stand the test and prove Himself to you.

Flood Tide

BLESSED TO BE MADE A BLESSING

Your heavenly Father says that if you will bring *all* your tithes and offerings, He will open the windows of heaven and pour out that flood of blessings upon you! Your Savior says that He will both give you seed to sow and multiply your seed sown. (2 Cor. 9:10.) He gives you both!

There are two vitally important things God wants to do in your life now: to *bless* you and to make you a *blessing* to others.

He wants you so blessed that all your needs are being met — spiritually, physically, and financially.

Most people want to be blessed, but they have never learned that God wants to *make* them a blessing. You can't be a blessing unless you are being blessed. When you are blessed, then you must further yield yourself to God so He can *make* you a *blessing.*

It takes His "making power" at work in your life, by your choice, for you to become a blessing. Ordinarily, you won't make yourself a blessing to others, but will use your blessings only on yourself.

Here's a word to help you:

Flood Tide

Without God, I cannot.
Without me, He will not.

God and you working together will do it!

You also have to choose to prove God to yourself. Make a quality decision that if you do what God says, He is provable. He will bless you by putting you in the flood stage; then out of the flood stage, He will make you a provable blessing through which many others will see God is a good God and will come to know Him for themselves.

You can't give something that you don't have. If you don't have it, you can't give it!

When God blesses you spiritually, then you want to be made a spiritual blessing to others.

When God blesses you in your spiritual body, you want to share the truth about God's healing power and be made a physical blessing to others.

When God blesses you financially, then it is your joy to be made a financial blessing to others.

Remember, being blessed doesn't automatically make you a blessing. Just as you must give God your *seed-faith* for Him to bless you, you must continue to plant and receive in order for God to continue to make you a blessing.

STEP INTO THE FLOOD

God desires you to come into a personal, daily relationship with Jesus so He can constantly keep the windows of heaven open to you, pouring out His blessings of deliverance upon you.

The earth can contain a little trickle of water. It can contain a stream of water. It can contain a river — even the mighty Mississippi! But the earth will never be able to contain a flood!

This is how God wants to bless you. He says, "I'll bless you where there is not room enough to contain it — not a trickle, not a stream, not a river, but a flood!"

A flood!

When you give your tithes and offerings as seeds of your faith, knowing Who God is and who you are, then you are walking out into that flood.

God will flood your life — spiritually, physically, and financially.

Flood Tide

In spite of setbacks, discouragement, attacks of illness, or any other attempt of the devil to destroy your life, you can walk with joy on your countenance and expectancy in your soul. You can take down your umbrella because the blessings of God are going to pour down on you! Flood stage is coming!

In Luke 6:38, Jesus said:

> *Give, and it shall be given unto you; good measure, pressed down, and shaken together, and running over, shall men give into your bosom.*

When something is "running over," it cannot be contained. Jesus completed His thought by saying:

> *For with the same measure that ye mete (give) withal it shall be measured to you again.*

The blessings of the Old Covenant did not die out with Jesus. He merely fulfilled the Old Covenant to give us a better one. (Heb. 8:6.) God blessed Abraham exceedingly, and that same blessing is in effect today — only it has been enlarged by our Lord Jesus Christ.

Give, and it shall be given to you.

How?

Flood Tide

Good measure, pressed down, shaken together, and running over. *Running over!* You can't contain it!

One story I have heard is about the person who decided to give to God according to this scripture. He took a teaspoon and measured out his giving. Then later on when he got in trouble, he called on God for a miracle.

But God said, "I can only do to you the way you do others. Give Me your teaspoon."

The man replied, "But, Lord, I need You to use a shovel!"

The Lord answered, "Then give with a shovel."

I have prayed for thousands and thousands of people, and I have discovered that many people I pray for want magic. They don't want to study the Word of God or hear the Word preached. They don't want to know Who God really is. They don't want to re-educate their minds not to trust in man's system which is as changeable and unreliable as the world, but learn to trust in God, Whose system never fails. They don't want to give to God. They just want a magic touch that they can take; then go and live any old way they want to live. They haven't learned yet that you don't get something for nothing — not even from God.

Why do I pray for them?

Because they are human beings. No matter how they live or what they do, I pray for them.

THE BLESSING WAY

But there is a better way: the *seed-faith* way, which is the blessing way.

There doesn't have to be a curse on your blessings. There can be a release of your blessings.

The windows of heaven should not be shut. They should be opened wide, pouring out those blessings — not a trickle, not a stream, not a river, but a flood!

You should give your tithes to the Lord, not because God needs them, but because you love God and need to plant a seed out of your need.

Where do *you* stand in relation to God's blessings?

Are you in the trickle? the stream? the river? Or are you in the flood stage: where you can't contain God's spiritual, physical, and financial blessings in your life and must share them with others.

Flood Tide

When you bring your tithes and offerings, you should always be expressing your awareness and knowledge of God as the most high God, possessor of heaven and earth, deliverer from all your enemies.

You should give your *tithes of all* to God because of Who He is . . . and because of who you are and what you need.

I CHALLENGE YOU

Now I issue a challenge to you as well as to myself: Let us make a decision to move from the trickle into the stream, from the stream into the river, then jump over into the flood!

Pray the flood to cover you up so that you can say:

"All my needs are met and overflowing. I've never felt so good in my life. I've got so much health that I want to go out and help somebody else get their health. God is so great! I have to tell somebody!

"God is the most high God, possessor of heaven and earth, deliverer from all my enemies. Therefore, I give tithes of all, and God is going to open the windows of heaven and pour out on me a blessing that I can't even contain.

Flood Tide

"God will take the curse off my blessings. He will bless me. I come with my love, with my justice, with my faith. I give tithes of everything as my *seed-faith* because God is my Source and He has commanded me to *prove* Him to bless me and make me a blessing."

Change the way you give. Think of it as a seed you sow for God to grow. Start looking for the open windows. Start expecting God to pour out a blessing you just cannot contain.

Expect God's healing power.

Expect God's spiritual power.

Expect God's financial power.

Expect a miracle!

Rejoice and let the blessings of the Lord be upon you!

Don't let a curse be on your blessings. Let the Lord open the windows of heaven to you and pour you out a blessing there is not room enough to contain!

Let the Lord put you into expectancy that you shall receive from Him, that you shall receive the blessings, that you shall receive the flood.

Let us be a prosperous and successful people in God!

Let us be an example of God's reality and goodness to all people!

Let us trust God as our Source of total supply, so that in good times and bad times, we know He will make a way where there is no way.

Let us serve God, for beside Him there is no other.

8
The Devourer Rebuked In Your Life

"And I will rebuke the devourer for your sakes . . ."
                    Malachi 3:11

Chapter 8
The Devourer Rebuked
In Your Life

When you return to God and bring to Him your seed of tithes and offerings to prove Him with them, you can expect those windows of heaven to be opened.

Then you can expect something else. In Malachi 3:11, God said:

> And I will rebuke the devourer for your sakes, and he shall not destroy the fruits of your ground; neither shall your vine cast her fruit before the time in the field, saith the Lord of hosts.

What is devouring lives in the world today?

Flood Tide

Sin.

Where does sin come from?

The devil.

Satan, the devil, is the devourer. In John 10:10, Jesus called him a thief. He said:

> *The thief cometh not, but for to steal, and to kill, and to destroy: I am come that they might have life, and that they might have it more abundantly.*

In Acts 10:38, Peter stated:

> *God anointed Jesus of Nazareth with the Holy Ghost and with power: who went about doing good, and healing all that were oppressed of the devil.*

The devil had oppressed the people and made them sick, but Jesus came and took that oppression from them.

Satan is the devourer, but God said, "I will rebuke the devourer. I will rebuke him from devouring, and I will do it for *your* sakes."

In the Gospel of Matthew as Jesus prepares to give us the New Covenant, He speaks to the

The Devourer Rebuked

multitude about the scribes and Pharisees. These were religious men who had taken the place of Moses. The scribes were men who hand-copied the Scriptures; the Pharisees were the "spiritual" leaders. They had declared themselves to be the chief descendants of Abraham.

In Matthew 23:4, the Lord Jesus takes these men to task. He says of them:

> For they bind heavy burdens and grievous to be borne, and lay them on men's shoulders; but they themselves will not move them with one of their fingers.

In the 14th verse, He says:

> Woe unto you, scribes and Pharisees, hypocrites! for ye devour widows' houses, and for a pretence make long prayer.

In verse 23, He says:

> Woe unto you, scribes and Pharisees, hypocrites! for ye pay tithe of mint and anise and cummin (seeds they planted), and have omitted the weightier

matters of the law, judgment, mercy, and faith: these ought ye to have done, and not to leave the other undone.

In other words, He is saying to them: "You have paid your tithes, but you have had no righteous judgment. You have given no mercy. You have not planted seeds of faith."

In verse 24, He calls them *blind guides, which strain at a gnat, and swallow a camel.*

When you do what God has said to do — when you bring in all the tithes and offerings — then *for your sake* He will rebuke the devourer. He will do it because of who you are.

You worship and give because of Who God is and God acts in your behalf because of who you are.

Who are you? The one who has returned to God, who has declared the name of Jesus to be above every name and your Deliverer, who continually presents to God all the tithes and offerings as seeds of your faith.

He has accepted your *seed-faith* toward Him, so you need to accept His miracle harvests toward you, to graciously receive from Him.

The Devourer Rebuked

God wants to bless you. He wants to rebuke the devourer from your life. Let Him!

Accept His flood of blessings.

Accept His rebuke of your enemies.

A man came to one of our meetings with a great financial need. He came to learn how to get into *seed-faith*. When he "heard" the word of faith preached on *giving/living,* he felt his faith "come" up within him to start giving out of his need, to plant seed for a harvest, and for God, his Source, to rebuke the devourers of his life.

That was his first time to plant his very best seeds, although they were small. He was one of the happiest men I had ever seen give to the Lord. And God did what He said He would do. In six months' time, God had blessed that man with $100,000 in cash!

When he began, he wasn't even in the trickle. But God took him through the trickle, through the stream, through the river, and into the flood. He couldn't contain God's blessings upon him!

I want you to know Who God is and who you are.

Flood Tide

I want you to get a good image of God.

I want you to feel good about yourself.

Never again say, "Poor little me."

Don't ever say, "I can't give anything."

Don't ever say, "I am nothing."

Say, "I know Who my God is and He knows who I am. He lets me prove Him by my seed plantings through giving my tithes and offerings. For my sake, He will rebuke the devourer in my life. People will call me a delightsome person." (Mal. 3:12.)

This is a most wonderful time to be talking about God pouring out His blessings upon us.

People who know Who God is and are willing and eager to give to God are candidates for the flood tide, for the running over, for the inexhaustible riches of Christ.

I praise God that each of us is now in the process of knowing in our hearts that God is opening the windows of heaven to us — to you and to me.

Because of this great truth of His Word, we are starting to put into faith in a rhythm of giving and

The Devourer Rebuked

receiving. God is starting to pour out a blessing we can't contain — a flood! We must not be satisfied with anything but that flood tide. The running over. The inexhaustible riches.

But we begin by knowing Who Jesus really is and what He is to us: He is the deliverer from all our enemies. He makes us kings and priests unto Him on this earth. He gives us the silver and the gold for our right purposes.

He enables us to believe Him to dispatch our angels and have them take our health, our joy, our money out of the devil's hands and bring it to us. God's people are beginning again to be blessed — and made a blessing.

In America there is unemployment, inflation, uncertainty. Fear about the financial situation is everywhere you turn.

Why?

Because people have forgotten — or never known — Who their Source is.

Do you believe that God is poor?

My friend, God is not poor. He is more than rich! He possesses the heavens and the earth. He owns all the silver and all the gold. He has a system that works.

Do you believe in Him and His system?

Are you His child and trusting Him as your Source?

If you are, then when you come to Him and worship Him with your tithes and offerings, planting them as your seeds of faith, start expecting your miracle of blessing, and to be made a blessing.

Don't be a slave to America's economy, or anything else.

As one in *seed-faith*, the devourer is rebuked by God from your life!

The windows of heaven are flung open to you!

Your Savior — the possessor of heaven and earth, Whose name is above every name, Who has put all things under His feet — is pouring out a flood of blessings — not a trickle, not a stream, not a river, but a flood!

Raise your sights now to live in flood-stage Christianity!

9
Christianity —
The Great Confession

Chapter 9
Christianity —
The Great Confession

Hebrews 3:1 states that Christ Jesus is the Apostle and High Priest of our profession (or confession). Christianity is often called "The Great Confession."

Words, based on our faith in God, are the most powerful things in the universe. We activate our faith in God through those words we speak forth.

As you obey the scriptures about planting your seeds of faith, you should confess aloud the truth of God's Word. When you do this, you are confessing Jesus Christ Himself, Who is the Word, and He Himself will actually produce what is promised.

Flood Tide

God's Word cannot return void because Jesus, the Word, is alive!

Using your full name, confess aloud this personal confession as your point of contact when you give your tithes and offerings as *seed-faith* to God. Enter into your *flood tide* of God's blessings!

Confession For Your Personal Flood Tide

I, _____, come to You, heavenly Father, in the all-powerful name of Jesus Christ of Nazareth and worship You with all my tithes and offerings of everything You have blessed me with.

I, _____, worship You as the most high God, the possessor of heaven and earth, the deliverer from all my enemies, the name that is above every name. You are my Source and the Supplier of all my resources — the God Who owns all the silver and gold.

Christianity — The Great Confession

    I,_____, thank You that I am planting my seed and am blessed exceedingly with the same blessings and multiplication of resources that came upon Abraham. I acknowledge You as the One Who makes me rich with all spiritual, physical, and financial blessings for all my need.

    I,_____, thank You now that the windows of heaven are opened to me and that You are now pouring out a blessing that there is not room enough for me to contain.

    I,_____, thank You that I am now getting into the flood tide of Your blessings — not a trickle, not a stream, not a river, but a flood!

    I,_____, thank You that I have entered into flood-stage Christianity!

Harrison House Presents

The Ministry Of Oral Roberts

Oral Roberts has a heart for the people — *all* people.

His concept of God and his personal vision for ministry have often been too big for some critics to accept. But it would be difficult to harshly criticize a man who has helped millions of people find salvation, receive healing for their bodies, see God as the Source of all that is good, and visualize hope for their futures.

The ministry of Oral Roberts began over 30 years ago when God spoke to him and said, "Bring the message of My healing power to your generation." Oral Roberts laid hands on the sick because God told him to.

Oral had known what sickness was. At 17 he had lain on his death bed for over a year, hemorrhaging from tuberculosis in both lungs. His sister Jewell brought him the words that would forever change the direction of his life: "Oral, God is going to heal you."

Soon after, Oral was carried to a tent meeting and prayed for. He was completely healed by the power of God.

Two months later he held his first evangelistic meeting.

For years Oral Roberts took the healing message across America and around the world. He entered into the homes and hearts of the people by television. His tent crusades were packed with people seeking a miracle from God.

Then God added another dimension, one that Oral had known from the beginning. He was to build a university to educate young men and women to go to the uttermost bounds of the earth for God. Their work would exceed Oral's. God showed him that success without a successor is failure.

Oral Roberts University with its outstanding academic record has been an overwhelming success. Although ORU was built by a man who was not an "educator," it is one of the finest universities in America, and much more: a charismatic center for the whole world.

Then God spoke to Oral a third time. He was to build a hospital, clinic, and research center: *The City of Faith*. This project is opening this November, the only medical and research center to merge God's healing streams of medicine and prayer. It is designed to serve over one million sick people a year, and to be the final training place for hundreds of healing teams to go to the nations.

Oral Roberts' vision for ministry may be too big for some people to understand, but it is certain that he is a man of God and God has never failed him.